Red Imported Fire Ants

Attacking Everything

by Meish Goldish

Consultant: Brian L. Fisher
Department of Entomology
California Academy of Sciences, San Francisco

BEARPORT PUBLISHING

New York, New York

Publisher: Kenn Goin
Editor: Jessica Rudolph
Creative Director: Spencer Brinker
Design: The Design Lab
Photo Researcher: Jennifer Zeiger

Library of Congress Cataloging-in-Publication Data

Goldish, Meish, author.
  Red imported fire ants : attacking everything / by Meish Goldish.
    pages cm. — (They don't belong : tracking invasive species)
    Audience: Ages 7–12.
  Includes bibliographical references and index.
  ISBN 978-1-62724-831-0 (library binding) — ISBN 1-62724-831-5 (library binding)
  1. Fire ants—Juvenile literature. 2. Insects—Juvenile literature. I. Title.
  QL568.F7G48 2016
  595.79'6—dc23
                              2015008814

For more information, write to Bearport Publishing Company, Inc., 45 West 21st Street, Suite 3B, New York, New York 10010. Printed in the United States of America.

10 9 8 7 6 5 4 3 2 1

Contents

A Texas Mystery 4

Invading America 6

Ant Colonies 8

Spreading Out 10

Fiery Stings 12

Dangerous Venom 14

Attacking Animals 16

Plant Killers 18

Electrical Attacks 20

Trying to Fight Back 22

Ants Versus Flies 24

Looking for Answers 26

Other Invasive Insects 28

Glossary 30

Bibliography 31

Read More 31

Learn More Online 31

Index 32

About the Author 32

A Texas Mystery

Small creatures called horned lizards once lived throughout Texas. They roamed the state searching for their favorite food, an **insect** called the harvester ant. Then, in the 1970s, something odd happened. Horned lizards began to disappear from Texas. Scientists were puzzled. What could have caused this?

Horned lizards have spikes all over their bodies to protect themselves from enemies.

Horned lizards need to eat lots of harvester ants (right) to survive.

Eventually, scientists discovered the problem—an **invasive species** called red **imported** fire ants. These insects gobbled up the seeds that harvester ants usually eat. With little food, harvester ants began to vanish. Horned lizards were then left without their main source of food.

In addition, groups of the fierce fire ants sometimes attacked and ate baby horned lizards. As a result, the number of lizards in Texas dropped sharply. Unfortunately, the tiny insects were also causing destruction in many other states.

A red imported fire ant

Red imported fire ants may be reddish brown or black. They are very small—only about $\frac{1}{8}$ inch (3.2 mm) long. That's about half the length of a pencil eraser.

Invading America

Red imported fire ants arrived in the United States by accident. How? In the 1930s, ships carrying goods sailed from South America to Mobile, Alabama. Ship workers in South America had loaded soil into the bottoms of the boats to keep them balanced at sea. However, they didn't know that red fire ants were living in the soil.

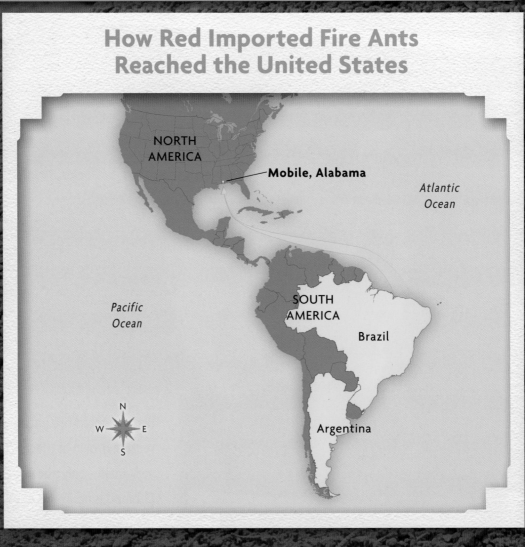

How Red Imported Fire Ants Reached the United States

NORTH AMERICA

Mobile, Alabama

Atlantic Ocean

Pacific Ocean

SOUTH AMERICA

Brazil

Argentina

Red imported fire ants originally came from Argentina and Brazil, in South America.

During the trip to the United States, the small ants spread all over the boats. When the ships reached Alabama, it didn't take long for the insects to crawl onto the shore. Then they began to build homes.

There are several kinds of fire ants that are **native** to the United States. The word *imported* was added to the name of the fire ants that came from South America.

Red imported fire ant

Red imported fire ants look similar to fire ants that are native to the United States, such as the Southern fire ant.

Southern fire ant

Ant Colonies

Like all kinds of ants, fire ants live together in a group called a **colony**. To build an underground nest for the group, **worker ants** dig tunnels under the ground and push soil up to the surface. Soon, dirt **mounds** start to form. Each mound may rise as high as 2 feet (6.1 m) above the ground!

Researchers examine a red imported fire ant colony mound.

After building a nest, the worker ants have other jobs to do. They guard their mounds from enemies. They also find food for the colony, which includes the **queen ant** and her young. A small colony may have only one queen. Larger colonies can have several queens. With each queen laying up to 1,500 eggs a day, a colony grows quickly.

A red imported fire ant queen (with wings) is much larger than the worker ants.

Red imported fire ants build nests on all kinds of land, including fields, lawns, and golf courses. One colony can have 500,000 ants.

Spreading Out

Over a few years, the population of red imported fire ants in Alabama grew. Soon, the insects spread to other locations. Some ants had help moving. People dug up the soil the ants lived in and transported it to plant **nurseries** in many states. Other ants marched to new areas on their own.

Red Imported Fire Ants in the United States

☐ States where red imported fire ants have been found

Today, red imported fire ants live throughout the South. They do not live in the northern United States because the weather gets too cold there, and they need warm weather to live.

Some ants moved when **floods** destroyed their underground homes. During a flood, thousands of worker ants join together. Using their bodies, they form a raft that floats on the water. The queen and her eggs are carried safely on top of the raft. Once the floating ants hit dry land, the workers build a new home.

Unlike most ants, red imported fire ants are able to survive floods by floating on the water in a group.

Fiery Stings

Wherever they go, red imported fire ants cause major problems. People who live in the South know the insects will attack anyone who disturbs their colony. If someone accidentally steps on a mound, hundreds of worker ants may **swarm** onto the person's skin.

A red imported fire ant attacking a person

During an attack, an ant first sinks its strong jaws into the skin of a **victim**, to get a firm hold. This bite hurts, but the stings that follow are much more painful. The fire ant stabs the victim several times with the sharp stinger at the tail end of its body. With every sting, the ant shoots **venom** into the person's body. The venom causes a terrible burning feeling, which is how the fire ant got its name.

stinger

jaws

When attacking victims, red imported fire ants are more **aggressive** than native fire ants. The imported ants' stings are also more painful.

Dangerous Venom

After a fire ant attack, a victim is left with itchy red patches and **pustules**. A person can usually recover quickly—unless the victim is **allergic** to the ant's venom. Then the person may become very ill. In rare cases, sting victims have even died.

Pustules ——

Most fire ant victims can treat their stings with soap, water, and ice. The skin must be kept clean, or it can become **infected**. A person should see a doctor if he or she develops **hives**, feels sick or dizzy, or has trouble breathing after being stung.

The Wingard family from Texas knows how dangerous red imported ants can be. One spring day in 1990 in the town of Anderson, fire ants stung two-year-old Ryan Wingard. The boy had been playing in his family's backyard. Soon, red blotches appeared on Ryan's body. His lips turned blue and his tongue swelled up. His mother saw that he couldn't breathe. Ryan was rushed to a hospital. Luckily, doctors were able to treat him quickly and save his life.

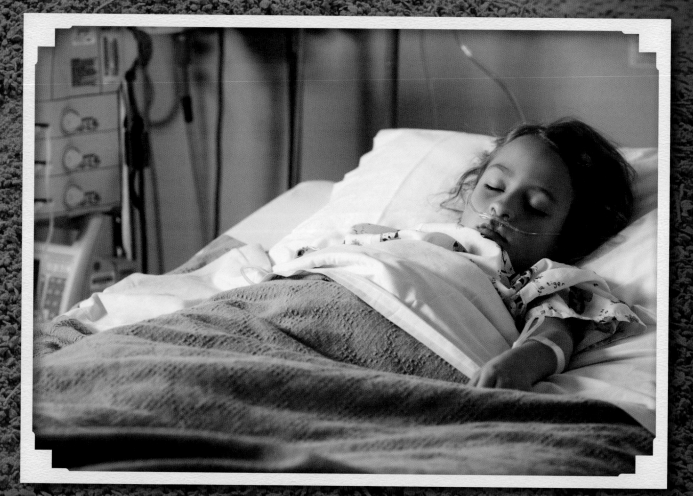

About five million Americans are stung by red imported fire ants each year. Thousands of victims have to be treated by doctors.

Attacking Animals

People are not the only targets of red imported fire ants. Animals can also become victims. The ants will do anything to protect their colony—even attack very large creatures, such as cows, that step on their mounds. Huge cows have been sent running in pain after being stung by fire ants.

Cattle are often attacked by fire ants.

Red imported fire ants also swarm over animals for another reason—food. The ants often target newborns because their venom can more easily kill small animals. Calves, fawns, and baby alligators are all at risk of becoming fire ant food. Sometimes, fire ants bite mother hens to drive them away from their nests. Then the ants attack, kill, and eat the mothers' young chicks.

After killing an animal, each ant tears off a chunk of the animal's skin. Then it takes the food home to feed the other ants in the colony.

These fire ants have killed a lizard.

Plant Killers

Like most ants, red imported fire ants are omnivores and eat both animals and plants. However, red imported fire ants do more harm to plants than most other kinds of ants. Fire ants **devour** many different kinds of crops, including cabbages, potatoes, and corn.

Fire ants swarming a plant

The fierce fire ants attack all parts of a plant. They tear apart stems and suck the liquid out of them. The ants bite into a plant's fruit and eat the seeds. They also kill fruit and nut trees by eating away at trunks and roots. This causes big problems for farmers. Every year, they lose millions of dollars in sales from destroyed crops.

Red imported fire ants often invade homes. They'll eat anything left sitting on a table or countertop, such as nuts, meat, and cheese.

Fire ants eating a scrap of food

Electrical Attacks

Red imported fire ants don't just attack living things. Strangely, they also attack electrical equipment! In cool weather, the ants sometimes nest inside televisions, light switches, or other devices that give off heat. This way, the insects are able to stay warm when it's cold outside. Often, the ants build nests in the equipment by bringing dirt inside them.

Red imported fire ants built a nest in this power box, located on the outside of a building.

Red imported fire ants have also been found living inside cars, trucks, boats, and airplanes.

Scientists aren't exactly sure why, but the insects sometimes bite and sting electrical wires inside the equipment. This can cause a device to stop working. Fire ants have damaged telephone wires and gasoline pumps. In Texas, red imported fire ants are the main cause for traffic lights to fail. This has even led to car accidents.

An exterminator, a person who gets rid of pests from buildings, destroyed a colony of ants that had been living inside this wall socket.

Trying to Fight Back

Because red imported fire ants are so harmful, scientists have tried different ways to get rid of them. In 1962, they began to spray a **pesticide** called mirex on fields and lawns. Scientists hoped the poison would wipe out the **foreign** insects. Oddly enough, the spray ended up helping the fire ants. How?

A plane spraying pesticides over a field

Red imported fire ants were strong enough to **resist** mirex. However, the poison killed weaker insects, including some native fire ants. As a result, the imported fire ants had fewer **competitors** for land to build their nests in and for food.

Pesticides can be extremely dangerous to animals and humans.

Over time, scientists found that mirex didn't just kill insects. It also killed other kinds of animals, including some birds. In 1978, the government outlawed the use of the pesticide.

WARNING
PESTICIDE USE
FOR INFORMATION CONTACT:
DATE POSTED
DATE SPRAYED

Ants Versus Flies

One person looking for ways to fix the red imported fire ant problem is Dr. Lawrence Gilbert, a scientist from Texas. During a visit to South America, he saw that the population of red fire ants is being controlled by tiny phorid flies.

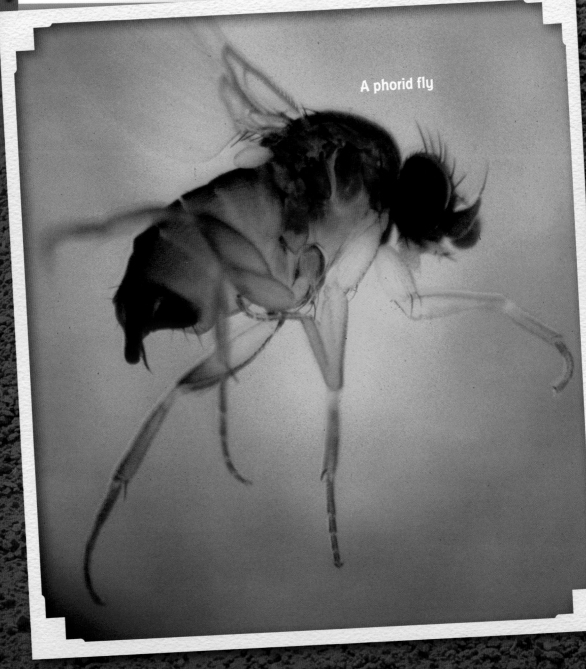

A phorid fly

A phorid fly uses a needlelike body part to pierce a fire ant and lay an egg inside its body. Soon, a fly **larva** hatches from the egg. Then the larva moves into the ant's head and grows. Not long after, the ant dies, and its head falls off. Then a young fly climbs out of the ant's head and flies away.

fly—

A young phorid fly hatches from the head of a red imported fire ant.

—ant head

If enough phorid flies lay eggs in ants' bodies, many fire ants can be killed. Dr. Gilbert is doing tests to see if phorid flies can help control the population of red imported fire ants in the United States.

Looking for Answers

Can phorid flies solve the problem of red imported fire ants? Possibly. However, first scientists need to answer some questions, like: Which species of phorid flies will work best against red imported fire ants? Will the flies attack native ant species?

A phorid fly hovers over red imported fire ants.

Also, not everyone wants red imported fire ants to disappear. Despite the harm they cause, the insects do some good. For example, they kill fleas and ticks. These pests can hurt dogs, cats, and even people.

Most scientists believe red imported fire ants will never be **eliminated** from the United States. Yet they hope to control the ants' population—and find ways for people to live with these aggressive creatures.

A boll weevil

Red imported fire ants also help farmers by attacking boll weevils and aphids. These pests can destroy cotton and sugarcane plants.

Other Invasive Insects

Here are four other kinds of foreign insects that cause problems in the United States.

Africanized Honeybees

- These bees were created when scientists brought African bees to Brazil in the 1950s to **mate** with honeybees. Some of the new bees escaped. By the 1990s, they had spread to the United States.

- Africanized honeybees, also known as killer bees, attack people and animals that disturb their beehives.

- People who are stung by a large number of Africanized honeybees can be seriously hurt, and some victims even die.

- In the United States, Africanized honeybees have stayed mostly in the South, because the weather in the North is too cold for them.

Argentine Ants

- These ants came to the United States on ships from South America in the late 1800s.

- Some Argentine ants build colonies under homes and inside them.

- Argentine ants do not sting, but they will bite if a person or animal disturbs them.

- Scientists have discovered "supercolonies" of Argentine ants. The supercolonies can stretch underground for hundreds or even thousands of miles.

Asian Longhorned Beetles

- These beetles came to the United States on ships from Asia in the 1990s.

- Asian longhorned beetles attack many kinds of trees, including maple, elm, willow, and birch. They have killed thousands of trees in New York, New Jersey, Massachusetts, Ohio, and Illinois.

- Trees that are **infested** with the beetles must be cut down and removed. Otherwise, the beetles will spread to and kill nearby trees.

Tawny Crazy Ants

- These ants came to the United States from South America in the early 2000s. They live in many of the same areas as red imported fire ants.

- Tawny crazy ants get their name from their butterscotch coloring and the way they behave. They often seem to run around crazily.

- Tawny crazy ants do not sting. However, they attack and kill many creatures with their jaws, such as other insects and spiders.

- Each ant produces an acid that it smears all over its body. The acid helps the crazy ant resist the venom of red imported fire ants. This allows the crazy ant to easily steal food from fire ants.

Glossary

aggressive (uh-GRESS-iv) threatening

allergic (uh-LUR-jik) having a condition that causes a person's body to react badly to something

colony (KOL-uh-nee) a large group of insects that live together

competitors (kom-PET-i-turz) animals that fight against each other for the same resources

devour (di-VOUR) eat hungrily and quickly

eliminated (ih-LIM-uh-nay-tid) gotten rid of; removed entirely

floods (FLUHDZ) overflows of water onto land that is not normally underwater

foreign (FOR-uhn) from another country

hives (HYEVZ) itchy rashes on the skin

imported (im-POR-tid) brought from one country to another

infected (in-FEK-tid) filled with harmful germs

infested (in-FESS-tid) filled with harmful creatures such as insects

insect (IN-sekt) a small animal that has six legs, three main body parts, two antennae, and a hard covering

invasive species (in-VAY-siv SPEE-sheez) plants or animals that have been moved from one place to another, where they do not belong

larva (LAR-vuh) a young insect that has a wormlike body

mate (MAYT) come together to have young

mounds (MOUNDZ) piles of dirt

native (NAY-tiv) naturally born and living in a particular place

nurseries (NUR-sur-eez) places where trees and plants are sold

pesticide (PESS-tuh-side) a chemical used to kill pests, such as harmful insects

pustules (PUHSS-choolz) bumps on the skin filled with pus

queen ant (KWEEN ANT) a female ant that rules a colony and lays eggs

resist (ri-ZIST) not be affected by

swarm (SWORM) to gather or move together in large numbers

venom (VEN-uhm) poison that some animals send into the bodies of other animals through a bite or sting

victim (VIK-tuhm) a person or animal who is hurt or killed

worker ants (WUR-kur ANTS) members of an ant colony that do work such as building homes and gathering food

Bibliography

Taber, Stephen Welton. *Fire Ants*. College Station, TX: Texas A&M University Press (2000).

Tschinkel, Walter R. *The Fire Ants*. Cambridge, MA: Belknap Press (2006).

University of Texas at Austin Fire Ant Project
http://web.biosci.utexas.edu/fireant/

Read More

Ang, Karen. *Inside the Ants' Nest (Snug as a Bug: Where Bugs Live)*. New York: Bearport (2014).

Aronin, Miriam. *The Ant's Nest: A Huge Underground City (Spectacular Animal Towns)*. New York: Bearport (2010).

Iasevoli, Brenda. *Ants! (TIME for Kids Science Scoops)*. New York: HarperCollins (2005).

Spilsbury, Richard, and Louise Spilsbury. *Ant Colonies (Animal Armies)*. New York: PowerKids Press (2013).

Learn More Online

To learn more about red imported fire ants, visit
www.bearportpublishing.com/TheyDontBelong

Index

Africanized honeybees 28

Alabama 6–7, 10

Argentine ants 28

Asian longhorned beetles 29

attacks on animals 5, 16–17, 28–29

attacks on electrical equipment 20–21

attacks on people 12–13, 14–15, 28

attacks on plants 18–19, 29

bites 12–13, 16–17, 21, 28

colony 8–9, 17, 20, 28

floating on water 11

Gilbert, Dr. Lawrence 24–25

harvester ants 4–5

horned lizards 4–5

mirex 22–23

native fire ants 7, 13, 23

phorid flies 24–25, 26

queen ants 9, 11

South America 6–7

spreading to other areas 6–7, 8–9, 10–11

stings 12–13, 14–15, 16–17, 21, 28–29

tawny crazy ants 29

Texas 4–5, 10, 15, 21, 24

venom 13, 14, 17

Wingard, Ryan 15

worker ants 8–9

About the Author

Meish Goldish has written more than 200 books for children. His book *Surf Dog Miracles* was a Children's Choices Selection in 2014. He lives in Brooklyn, New York.